ARTEMIS FOWL

THE GRAPHIC NOVEL

Adapted by

EOIN COLFER
&
ANDREW DONKIN

Art by GIOVANNI RIGANO
Color by PAOLO LAMANNA

HYPERION BOOKS FOR CHILDREN
New York

How does one describe Artemis Fowl?
Various psychiatrists have tried and failed. The main problem is Artemis's own intelligence. He bamboozles every test thrown at him. He has puzzled the greatest medical minds and sent many of them gibbering to their own hospitals.

There is no doubt that Artemis is a child prodigy. But why does someone of such brilliance dedicate himself to criminal activities? This is a question that can be answered by only one person. And he delights in not talking.

Perhaps the best way to create an accurate picture of Artemis is to tell the by now famous account of his first villainous venture. I have put together this report from firsthand interviews with the victims, and as the tale unfolds you will realize that this was not easy.

This story began several years ago at the dawn of the twenty-first century. Artemis Fowl had devised a plan to restore his family's fortune. A plan that could topple civilizations and plunge the planet into a cross-species war.

He was twelve years old at the time. . . .

Of course, it had started with the Internet.
But then it always does.

Alien abductions. UFO sightings. Ley lines. Ancient stone circles.

And the People. It always came back to the People.

Trawling through gigs of data, he had compiled a database from the thousands of references to fairies he'd found from countries all over the world.

Each human civilization had its own term for the People. But there was no doubt that the reports referred to the same hidden race.

Many stories whispered of a special book carried by each fairy.

It was their Bible, containing the history of their race. It also contained their laws, their rules... and their weaknesses.

Any human who came into possession of such a book would have an entirely new species to exploit.

Of course, this book was said to be written in Gnommish, so even if someone could steal a copy, it would be of absolutely no use to any human.

CHAPTER 1:
THE BOOK

At least, any ordinary human...

I HOPE THIS ISN'T ANOTHER WILD-GOOSE CHASE, *BUTLER.*

ESPECIALLY AFTER OUR LITTLE MISHAP IN CAIRO.

NO, SIR. I'M CERTAIN THIS TIME. NGUYEN IS A GOOD MAN.

Ho Chi Minh City in the summer. Or Saigon, as the locals still called it. Sweltering by anyone's standards.

There seems no end to the crowds. Even the alleyways are full to bursting. Cooks smile and drop fish heads into woks of hissing oil. There's a new smell on every corner.

HMM, AFTER SIX FALSE ALARMS SPREAD OVER THREE CONTINENTS, I HOPE SO.

I BELIEVE THE CAFÉ IS LEFT AT THE NEXT JUNCTION, SIR.

A TABLE FOR SOME TEA, SIR? I'LL BE YOUR WAITER.

YOU ARE WEARING A SILK SHIRT AND THREE GOLD SIGNET RINGS. YOUR ENGLISH HAS A TINGE OF OXFORD ABOUT IT AND YOUR NAILS HAVE THE SOFT SHEEN OF HAVING BEEN RECENTLY MANICURED. YOU ARE NOT A WAITER. YOU, SIR, ARE OUR CONTACT.

SIT DOWN, *NGUYEN*.

IF YOUR PATHETIC WAITER DISGUISE WAS AN ATTEMPT TO CHECK FOR WEAPONS THEN I AM HAPPY TO TELL YOU THAT I AM UNARMED.

HOWEVER, BUTLER HERE IS CARRYING A PISTOL, TWO SHRIKE THROWING KNIVES, A DERRINGER, A GARROTTE WIRE, AND THREE STUN GRENADES.

DON'T FORGET THE COSH, SIR.

OH, YES, AND THE COSH.

I KNOW WHERE YOU CAN FIND WHAT YOU ARE SEARCHING FOR.

EXPLAIN.

"This woman. She is a healer, near Tu Do Street. She heals in exchange for rice wine. All the time, drunk. She is what you seek, Mister... Master Fowl."

AND NOW YOU'LL TAKE US TO HER.

NO, NO. INFORMATION ONLY. THAT WAS THE AGREEMENT. I DON'T WANT A CURSE ON MY HEAD.

I'M SORRY, MR. NGUYEN, BUT THE TIME WHEN YOU HAD A CHOICE IN THESE MATTERS IS LONG PAST.

"If you have brought us to the end of our quest, Mr. Nguyen, you will be well rewarded. If you have wasted our time, I am afraid Butler will not be pleased."

IT SEEMS WE MUST PROCEED ON FOOT. RUN IF YOU LIKE, BUT EXPECT A SHARP AND FATAL PAIN BETWEEN YOUR SHOULDER BLADES IF YOU DO.

"Don't worry I won't run."

SHE'S UNDER THERE. SHE NEVER GOES OUT. NOT EVEN TO BUY RICE SPIRITS.

BUTLER, THE GOGGLES PLEASE.

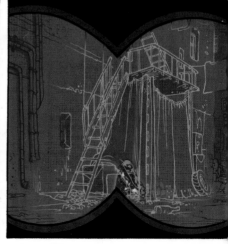

The gift of tongues.

Check.

MADAM, I HAVE A PROPOSITION FOR YOU.

Aversion to light.

Check.

GIVE ME DRINK.

PLEASE PAY OUR FRIEND, BUTLER. IN FULL.

AND, REMEMBER, MR. NGUYEN, THIS STAYS JUST BETWEEN US.

MY LIPS ARE SEALED.

"They had better be. Or Butler here will seal them permanently."

NOW, MADAM, TO BUSINESS. I MUST CONFESS, I DO NOT WANT HEALING. APART FROM A SLIGHT ALLERGY TO DUST MITES, I AM PERFECTLY HEALTHY.

NO, WHAT I WANT FROM YOU IS YOUR BOOK.

YOU WANT BOOK? GO LIBRARY.

YOU ARE NO HEALER. YOU ARE A SPRITE, A FAIRY, A KA-DALUN. AND I WANT YOUR BOOK.

IF YOU KNOW ABOUT THE BOOK, HUMAN, THEN YOU KNOW I HAVE ENOUGH MAGIC IN ME TO KILL YOU WITH A SNAP OF MY FINGERS!

I THINK NOT. LOOK AT YOU. YOU'RE NEAR DEAD. DRINK HAS RUINED YOU. I CAN SAVE YOU... IN RETURN FOR *THE BOOK.*

SAVE ME? EVEN A FAIRY TETHERED TO THE HUMAN REALM WILL OUTLIVE YOU, HUMAN.

NOT WITH HALF A PINT OF HOLY WATER INSIDE THEM.

LISTENING NOW, ARE WE? HERE'S THE DEAL. YOU GIVE ME YOUR PRECIOUS BOOK FOR THIRTY MINUTES, AND I SAVE YOUR LIFE. AND AFTER THAT, AS A BONUS, I'LL RETURN YOUR FAIRY MAGIC.

RETURN MY MAGIC? NOT POSSIBLE.

"One is spring water from a fairy well. That will counteract the holy water."

"The other contains a virus that feeds on alcohol. It will flush you clean."

WELL? DO WE HAVE A DEAL?

"Thirty of your minutes, human. No more."

MAKE SURE YOU PHOTOGRAPH EVERY PAGE. AND E-MAIL THE IMAGES HOME AS SOON AS YOU'RE DONE.

OF COURSE, SIR.

"No use to you anyway.

"Written in the old tongue."

YOUR NEEDLES HAVE STRONG MAGIC.

I'M AFRAID THE AMNESIAC MIXED INTO THE SECOND INJECTION MEANS THAT YOU WON'T REMEMBER US.

GOOD.

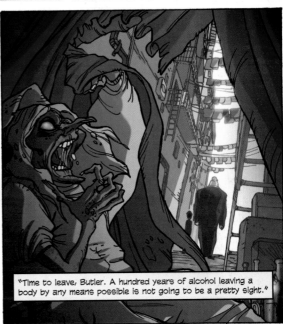

"Time to leave, Butler. A hundred years of alcohol leaving a body by any means possible is not going to be a pretty sight."

"Thank you, madam.

"It's been a pleasure doing business with you."

NAME:
Artemis Fowl the Second

CLASSIFICATION:
VERY DANGEROUS

KNOWN PSEUDONYMS AND ALIASES:
Dr. F. Roy Dean Schlippe, Stefan Bashkir,
Emmsey Squire

SPECIALIZED SKILLS:
Possibly possesses the greatest human intellect
of his generation

Perhaps any generation, but you can't believe everything he says.

NAME:
Butler

FIRST NAME:
D CENSORED

CLASSIFICATION:
Bodyguard

BACKGROUND:
The Butlers have been serving the Fowls for centuries.
Several eminent linguists believe this is how the noun originated.

SPECIALIZED SKILLS:
SAS-level marksmanship, martial arts including Cos Ta'pa, emergency
medicine, information technology, and Cordon Bleu cooking. The subject
is fluent in several languages. Believed to have studied extensively
under the Japanese sensei Madame Ko. Spent several years working
freelance in the espionage arena, including stints for the British
and French secret service.

DISTINGUISHING FEATURES:
Blue diamond tattoo on shoulder

WEAPON OF CHOICE:
Sig Sauer

KNOWN ALIASES:
Constantin Bashkir, Colonel Xavier Lee

KNOWN RELATIONS:
Juliet—younger sister
"The Major"—his uncle, believed to have been killed when the CENSORED

FOWL MANOR. IRELAND. DAYS LATER.

The Book is proving more stubborn than I anticipated.

CHAPTER 2:
TRANSLATION

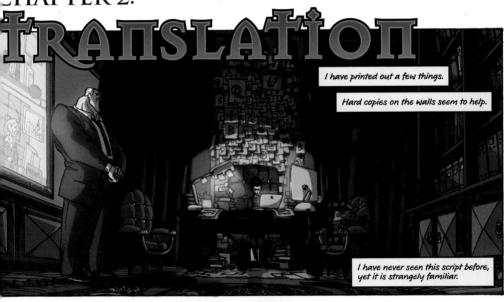

I have printed out a few things.

Hard copies on the walls seem to help.

I have never seen this script before, yet it is strangely familiar.

...And so Chicago's district attorney had to watch yet again as Mr. Spiro walked free from court. Problems here proving difficult to solve.

The text meanders around the page in no apparent order.

Juliet. Butler's little sister.

ARTEMIS? IT'S...IT'S MRS. FOWL. SHE'S ASKING FOR... SOMEONE.

Mother. I leave the computer comparing every symbol in the Book with every letter in every modern language in the entire world.

I don't think it's going to work.

MOTHER? ARE YOU AWAKE?

OF COURSE, I'M AWAKE. HOW CAN I SLEEP IN THIS BLINDING GLARE?

NEGATIVE

ARTEMIS, DARLING, WHERE HAVE YOU BEEN?

SCHOOL TRIP, MOTHER. SKIING IN AUSTRIA.

NEGATIVE

WOULD YOU CLOSE THOSE WRETCHED CURTAINS? THE LIGHT IS INTOLERABLE.

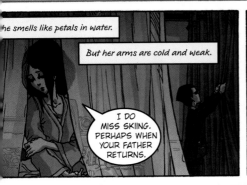

She smells like petals in water.

But her arms are cold and weak.

I DO MISS SKIING. PERHAPS WHEN YOUR FATHER RETURNS.

...EAR THINGS. AT NIGHT. THEY CRAWL ...NG THE PILLOWS AND INTO MY EARS. ...AREN'T OPEN THE CURTAINS OR I'D SEE THEM TOO.

MOTHER, I...

AND STOP CALLING ME "MOTHER." I DON'T KNOW WHO YOU ARE, BUT YOU'RE CERTAINLY NOT MY LITTLE ARTY.

DO YOU HEAR THEM? THEY'RE COMING FOR ME. THEY'RE EVERYWHERE.

NOW, GET OUT AND DON'T COME BACK OR I'LL HAVE MY HUSBAND TAKE CARE OF YOU. HE'S A VERY IMPORTANT MAN, YOU KNOW.

"Send that girl back up with the cucumber slices. And make sure they're clean this time."

Egyptian.

The first written human stories were about fairies, suggesting that their civilization predated man's. It would seem that the Egyptians had simply adapted an existing script to create their own.

I feel a tightness of anticipation in my chest. Unusual.

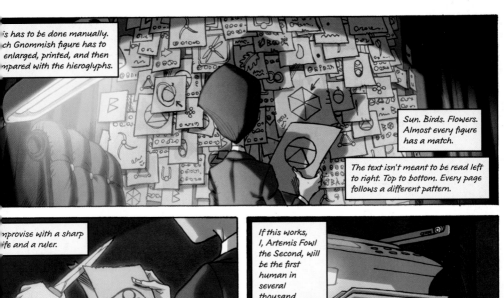

is has to be done manually. ch Gnommish figure has to enlarged, printed, and then mpared with the hieroglyphs.

Sun. Birds. Flowers. Almost every figure has a match.

The text isn't meant to be read left to right. Top to bottom. Every page follows a different pattern.

mprovise with a sharp ife and a ruler.

Then scan it in and press DECODE.

If this works, I, Artemis Fowl the Second, will be the first human in several thousand years to decode the magical words.

If:

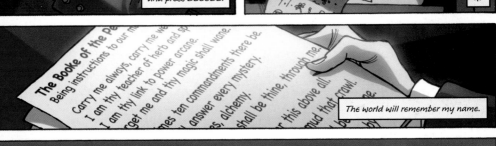

The Booke of the P

Being instructions to our m

Carry me always, carry me we

I am thy teacher of herb and sp

I am thy link to power arcane.

rget me and thy magic shall wane.

mes ten commandments there be.

answer every mystery.

es, alchemy.

shall be thine, through me.

r this above all.

ud that crawl.

The world will remember my name.

BUTLER, GET JULIET AND COME UP HERE. WE HAVE A LOT OF RATHER DIFFICULT JIGSAWS TO ASSEMBLE.

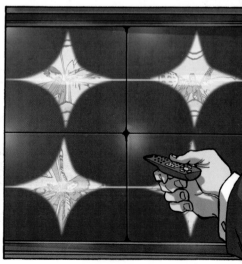

TO RENEW THEIR MAGIC, THEY MUST PICK A SEED FROM AN ANCIENT OAK TREE BY THE BEND IN A RIVER DURING A FULL MOON.

THE LEPRECHAUN BOUND BY CERTAIN RITUALS. RY SPECIFIC RITUALS THAT I HINK WE CAN USE TO TRACK ONE DOWN.

ARTEMIS, THE HING IS...WELL, LEPRECHAUNS. OU KNOW THEY'RE NOT REAL, DON'T YOU?

I TAKE IT, THEN, BUTLER HASN'T ALREADY TALKED TO YOU ABOUT THIS?

TRUST ME, JULIET. FAIRIES NOT ONLY EXIST, BUT WITH THE INFORMATION YOU TWO HAVE HELPED ME TRANSLATE, FAIRIES ARE ABOUT TO HELP ME RESTORE THE FINANCIAL FORTUNE AND THE CRIMINAL REPUTATION OF THE FOWL FAMILY...

ALL WE HAVE TO DO NOW IS CAPTURE ONE.

NAME:
Artemis Fowl Senior

FAMILY MOTTO:
Aurum potestas est (Gold is power.)

BACKGROUND:
Head of a criminal empire that stretched from Dublin's docklands
to the backstreets of Tokyo. Fowl Senior also had ambitions to
establish himself as a legitimate businessman.

KNOWN RELATIONS:
Angeline Fowl—wife and mother of Artemis Fowl II

RECENT HISTORY:
Bought a cargo ship and stocked it with 250,000 cans of cola and
set course for Murmansk in northern Russia. The ship, the Fowl
Star, was sunk in the Bay of Kola by a stolen Stinger missile fired
by the Russia Mafiya. Artemis Fowl Senior was reported missing,
presumed dead. CENSORED ORED in a ravine south of the harbor.

I wake up and it's one of those mornings when I can't quite decide what's annoying me most.

Is it my stick-in-the-mud sexist boss?

Or the fact that I still haven't made time to do the Ritual? Or the fact that I know I really should have?

CHAPTER 3:
HOLLY

With the goblin-dwarf turf war flaring up again, I'm going to need all the magic I can get.

Once upon a time, the uniform would have earned you some respect. Not anymore.

Now you're a target for every goblin that ever breathed a fireball.

Every goblin. Every gang member. Every lowlife and dirtbag under the earth.

God, I love this job.

I'm damn good at it too.

Except when...

Except...

HAMBURG.

POLIZEI

I'm the only female in Recon, and no one is going to drive me out. No one.

UNDERGROUND. DEEP UNDERGROUND.

The last human-free zone.

Since the humans began experimenting with mineral drilling, more and more fairies had been driven out of the shallow forts and into the depth and security of Haven City.

By human standards, Haven City is barely more than a small town—just ten thousand inhabitants.

In fairy terms though, Haven is the largest metropolis since the original Atlantis. And it's just as overcrowded and underserviced.

LOWER ELEMENTS POLICE STATION.

I'm in Recon. An elite branch of the police. We track runaway fairies to the surface and bring them back.

Mulch—kleptomaniac dwarf. Pickpocket. Master thief.

The junior officer doesn't know what he's got.

OFFICER SHORT.

HELLO, *MULCH.* YOU WANT TO ROLL UP YOUR SLEEVE?

HOW DID YOU...

HEY! THAT'S MY WATCH!

I CAN'T HELP MYSELF. IT'S MY NATURE.

And it's our nature to put him in a cell.

If I can just get past Root's office without...

SHORT! GET IN HERE!

COMMANDER ROOT

WELL?

They call him "Beetroot."

WHAT TIME DO YOU CALL THIS??

There's an office betting pool running on how long it'll be before his heart explodes.

SIR, I'M 45 SECONDS LATE.

Half the shift isn't even out of bed yet.

I KNOW WHAT YOU'RE THINKING, SHORT: WHY'S HE ALWAYS PICKING ON ME?

I'LL TELL YOU WHY. IT'S BECAUSE YOU'RE A GIRL.

BUT NOT FOR THE REASONS THAT YOU THINK. YOU ARE THE FIRST GIRL IN RECON. EVER. THERE ARE A LOT OF HOPES RIDING ON YOU.

IF YOU STAY, YOU HAVE TO BE THE BEST, SHORT. THE *BEST*.

EVER SINCE HAMBURG, I HAVEN'T BEEN SURE THAT YOUR BEST IS GOING TO BE GOOD ENOUGH.

HAMBURG.

SIR, APART FROM THE HAMBURG THING, MY RECORD SPEAKS FOR ITSELF. TEN SPOTLESS RECONS. SIR, PLEASE GIVE ME ANOTHER CHANCE.

IF I WAS ONE OF YOUR PRECIOUS SPRITES, WE WOULDN'T EVEN BE HAVING THIS CONVERSATION.

DON'T YOU DARE IMPLY...

Too far.

INCOMING EMERGENCY TRANSMISSION. PRIORITY ONE!

Commander Root, we have an emergency. We have a runner. Southern Italy. No shield. Human contact in minutes.

The bad news— it's a rogue troll.

Trolls are the meanest of the deep-tunnel creatures. They wander the labyrinth, preying on anything unlucky enough to cross their path.

Their tiny brains have no room for rules or restraint. Very occasionally, one gets to the surface. When they do, it's a disaster.

YOU RUNNING HOT?

I'm so far behind with the Ritual that I can't remember how long it's been. But if I say that, I'm finished. I nod and I lie.

BE CAREFUL WHAT YOU WISH FOR, OFFICER SHORT. LOOKS LIKE YOU GOT YOUR CHANCE. LOCATE THE TROLL. THEN WAIT—I SAID WAIT—FOR THE RETRIEVAL TEAM. GOT THAT?

"You ever seen what an angry troll can do to flesh and bone?"

"No, sir."

"Good. Keep it that way. Now, move."

OPS—the nerve center of Recon.

Run by Foaly, our resident centaur genius. Known for wearing tin hats so human intelligence agencies can't read his mind. Go figure.

THIS IS DOUBLE-LAYERED NOW. NO ONE KNOWS WHAT'S GOING ON IN MY HEAD.

THAT IS CERTAINLY TRUE.

Most centaurs are paranoid like this maybe because there aren't many of them left.

GOOD TO SEE YOU, HOLLY.

YOU, TOO.

HUMMINGBIRD Z spread your WINGS

I'M UNDER ORDERS TO GET YOU UP TO THE SURFACE *ASAP*. EVERYTHING'S READY...

"Helmet with live feed. Nuclear battery. No time limit.

"Locator— you find him. We find you. Routine stuff."

"Neutrino 2000 blaster— latest model. Three settings —scorched, well done, and crisped to a cinder.

"Dragonfly Wings— old model I'm afraid. Everything newer is already out on patrol."

My pod looks like an antique.

WHAT'S THAT... GRAY STAIN?

BRAIN FLUID. WE HAD A PRESSURE LEAK ON THE LAST MISSION. IT'S FIXED NOW THE OFFICER SURVIVED. UNFORTUNATELY FOR HIM.

Transport to the surface is via titanium pod. They have their own motors, but for an emergency speed ride like I need, you get dropped into a magma flare.

Great.

They call it "Riding the Hotspots."

"Get ready to fly, Short."

Moths flutter in the starlight.

Crickets chirp in the rough grass.

The breeze is fresh and strong.

How had the People ever left the surface?

The locator beeps.

I move.

I turn on my shield so I'm invisible to humans.

And to trolls.

The shield takes more out of me than I expect.

I should have done the Ritual.

I really, really should have done the Ritual.

CONTROL, DO YOU READ ME? *SITUATION CRITICAL!* HUMAN CONTACT IN SECONDS! I'M GOING IN.

Negative. Hold your position. You do not have an invitation to enter human premises.

Root's right. If I go into a human dwelling without an invitation, I lose all my magic.

But there are children in there. I have to do something.

AIUTO!

"Help." An invitation. At a stretch

It's always like this in the beginning. First there's the shocked silence.

Then comes the screaming.

With my shield on, no one can see me. Including Mr. Ugly.

I flick my weapon up to full power and hit the weak spot at the base of his skull.

e gets angry. eally angry.

No panic. He can't see me.

He can see me.

So can everyone else.

Fuel from my wing unit starts a fire. How can this get any worse?

Shield down. Magic gone.

It'll kill me, then slaughter everyone else.

Needlelike claws scrape at my ribs.

I can smell its breath. Greasy molars try and grip my helmet.

Helmet.

That's it.

The tunnel lights. High beams.

Eat this.

The shock finally gets through to his tiny brain. He goes down.

I put the fire out. Now all that's wrong is that I'm one hundred percent visible to forty human beings.

SCUSATEMI TUTTI. GUARDATE.

Not good.

Ribs hurt even worse than my head.

It's a shambles.

I'm just thinking how Root will skin me alive for this, when things go kind of fuzzy.

"Captain Short."

HOLLY?

WHAT IN THE NAME OF SANITY HAPPENED HERE?! YOU DISOBEYED MY DIRECT ORDER!!

YOU KNOW IT'S FORBIDDEN TO ENTER A HUMAN BUILDING WITHOUT AN INVITATION.

SIR, I DID GET INVITED IN. A CHILD CALLED FOR HELP.

YOU'RE ON SHAKY GROUND THERE, SHORT, AND YOU KNOW IT.

WE SAW THE WHOLE THING THROUGH YOUR HELMET CAMERA. WHAT HAPPENED TO YOUR SHIELD??

< THIS EVENING I HAVE ENJOYED A LOVELY MEAL WITH NOTHING UNUSUAL HAPPENING DURING THE COURSE OF THE EVENING AT ALL. >

I...

LIED TO ME, DIDN'T YOU? YOU HAVEN'T COMPLETED THE RITUAL FOR YEARS. YOU DO IT TONIGHT, SHORT. TONIGHT!

WE'LL TALK 'BOUT THIS SHAMBLES WHEN YOU GET BACK. MEANWHILE...

WELL DONE ON THE LIFE-SAVING THING. THIS COULD HAVE BEEN WORSE, AN AWFUL LOT WORSE.

< I WOULD CERTAINLY RECOMMEND THIS LOVELY RESTAURANT TO ALL MY FAMILY AND FRIENDS. >

"Now get out of here and get that Ritual done. You think you can do that, Short? Without getting into any more trouble I mean?"

I give him a look and tell him that I think I can manage that.

NAME:
Captain Holly Short

CLASSIFICATION:
Elf. Also first and only female Recon officer assigned to the LEPrecon—
an elite branch of the Lower Elements Police

BACKGROUND:
Subject is a city elf born and bred in Haven City. Like all elves,
she has the fairy powers of healing, the <u>mesmer</u>, shielding (from
human sight), as well as the gift of tongues.

CAREER:
Top pilot in her class at the Academy, where she studied under Wing
Commander Vinyáya. Worked traffic detail (nicknamed Wheelies) for
six months. Earned her silver acorns during highly controversial
initiation on the island of Tern Mor, off the Irish coast CENSORED
CENSORED ENSORED RED Turnball Root. CENSORED
Her early career in Recon was blighted by the notorious "Hamburg
Incident." A CENSORED fled to the surface and attempted to bargain
with a group of sinister human occultists who were using CENSORED
The cross-species fallout from Holly's intervention resulted in four
full memory wipes, one time-stop, and several cases of permanent
insanity among the humans involved. [Also see the classified Section
Eight CENSORED "The Hamburg Incident: Applied Evil."]

WEAPON OF CHOICE:
Neutrino3000

CHAPTER 4:
ABDVCTION

ONE HOUR AGO.

I head for the old country.

Butler prepares the field kit.

Mirrored sunglasses. Two pairs.

Portable radar.

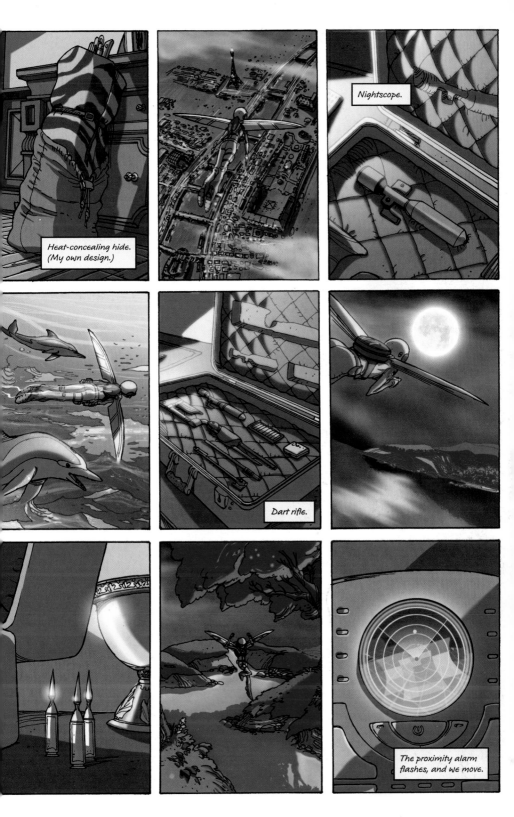

Heat-concealing hide.
(My own design.)

Nightscope.

Dart rifle.

The proximity alarm
flashes, and we move.

NOW.

River bend. Ancient oak.
Full moon. Perfect.

I'm under fire. How?

I'LL TAKE
THE PEASHOOTER,
MISS.

STAY BACK,
HUMAN. YOU DON'T
KNOW WHAT YOU'RE
DEALING WITH.

I BELIEVE,
FAIRY, THAT YOU
ARE THE ONE
UNFAMILIAR WITH
THE FACTS.

Fairy? He knows
I'm a fairy.

I HAVE
ENOUGH MAGIC
TO TURN YOU INTO
A PILE OF PIG
DROPPINGS.

IF YOU
ALREADY HAD MAGIC,
YOU WOULDN'T BE HERE
TO REPLENISH IT WITH
THE RITUAL.

He knows about the Ritual. This
is disastrous. This is catastrophic

I do have enough magic left for a *mesmer*.

HUMAN, YOUR WILL IS MINE.

I DON'T THINK SO.

A female. I hadn't expected that.

BUTLER?

SIR?

NICE SHOOTING.

"Let's get her back to the car."

NAME:
Fowl Manor

LOCATION:
A two-hundred-acre estate on the outskirts of Dublin, Ireland

BACKGROUND:
Records show the original Fowl castle was built by Lord Hugh Fowl
in the fifteenth century. It overlooks low-lying land on all sides.
Over the centuries, the castle was remodeled until it became the
manor that stands today. Fowl Manor has survived war, civil unrest,
and several tax audits.

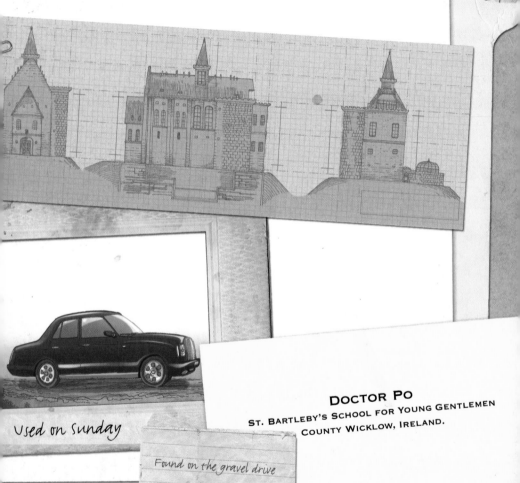

Used on Sunday

Found on the gravel drive

DOCTOR PO
ST. BARTLEBY'S SCHOOL FOR YOUNG GENTLEMEN
COUNTY WICKLOW, IRELAND.

IRELAND.

THIS FAIRY HARDWARE IS IMPRESSIVE, BUTLER.

WE COULD STOP THE MISSION RIGHT NOW, AND STILL MAKE A FORTUNE IN NEW PATENTS.

THIS HELMET SEEMS TO HAVE A LOCATOR BUILT INTO IT. NO DOUBT OUR GUEST'S COMRADES ARE TRACKING US RIGHT NOW.

RIGHT NOW, SIR?

THAT JAPANESE WHALER IS STILL TIED UP IN THE DOCK, ISN'T SHE, BUTLER?

I THINK IT'S TIME WE TAUGHT OUR DIMINUTIVE FRIENDS A LITTLE LESSON.

HAPTER 5:

MISSING IN ACTION

HAVEN CITY.

THE ROGUE TROLL IS DOWN IN A HOLDING CELL. WHAT'S THIS ABOUT, FOALY?

WE'VE LOST CONTACT WITH CAPTAIN SHORT.

PROBABLY EQUIPMENT MALFUNCTION. MAYBE YOU'RE NOT THE GENIUS YOU THINK YOU ARE.

THE EQUIPMENT DIDN'T MALFUNCTION. TAKE A LOOK AT THE FEED FROM HOLLY'S HELMET UNIT.

SHE'S CROSSED THE ALPS, FLOWN HIGH OVER PARIS — THEN THERE'S DOLPHINS — UNTIL THE IRISH COASTLINE.

SHE LOOKS FOR MAGICAL HOTSPOTS, LANDS, THEN THINGS SUDDENLY GO WRONG...

THE HELMET ENDS UP LENS DOWN IN THE MUD, BUT WE'VE STILL GOT SOUND. LISTEN...

THAT'S A HUMAN VOICE. THIS IS BAD.

If you already had magic, you wouldn't be here to replenish it with the Ritual.

DUBLIN DOCKS.

"A diversion then, Butler. Two minutes are all I need."

EVENING, LADIES. ISN'T IT A BIT LATE FOR BLOUSE-WEARING GIRLS LIKE YOU TO BE OUT? DO YOUR MOTHERS KNOW? OR ARE THEY TOO DRUNK BY THIS TIME OF NIGHT?

AND HERE'S THE WORST BIT.

IT GETS WORSE?

JUST BEFORE HOLLY DROPS THE HELMET, THERE'S A GLINT OF LIGHT IN THE FRAME. I SLOWED DOWN THE IMAGE. LOOK...

"Oh no."

POLICE!

EEEEEEEEEEE!
EEEEEEEEEEE!

TELL ME WE STILL HAVE HER LOCATOR SIGNAL?

LOUD AND CLEAR. GOT A STRONG SIGNAL MOVING NORTH AT ABOUT EIGHTY KLICKS AN HOUR.

GO TO FULL ALERT. GET RETRIEVAL OUT OF THEIR BUNKS AND PREP THEM FOR A SURFACE SHOT.

I WANT FULL TACTICAL AND A COUPLE OF TECHIES. YOU TOO, FOALY. WE MAY HAVE TO STOP TIME ON THIS ONE.

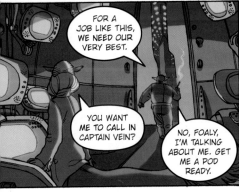

FOR A JOB LIKE THIS, WE NEED OUR VERY BEST.

YOU WANT ME TO CALL IN CAPTAIN VEIN?

NO, FOALY, I'M TALKING ABOUT ME. GET ME A POD READY.

"I'm leaving on the next magma flare."

HELLO?

YOU AWAKE, THEN?

MUMMLP.

I THOUGHT THE DART MIGHT HAVE KILLED YOU. ALIENS AND THOSE SORTS HAVE DIFFERENT INSIDES THAN US, DON'T THEY? I SAW THAT ON TELEVISION.

WHERE AM I? WHERE ARE MY THINGS?

ARTEMIS HAD TO TAKE YOUR LITTLE GUN AWAY.

"ARTEMIS"?

ARTEMIS FOWL. THIS WAS ALL HIS IDEA.

For some reason, even the name makes me shiver. Bad omen. Fairy intuition is never wrong.

YOU ARE A VERY PRETTY HUMAN...

WHY, THANK YOU.

I BET YOUR EYES ARE SPECTACULAR. IF ONLY I COULD SEE THEM...

I'LL TAKE MY GLASSES OFF FOR YOU AND THEN...

...AND THEN YOU CAN NAIL ME WITH THE *MESMER*. JUST HOW STUPID DO YOU THINK I AM?

As I sit back, I feel something digging into my ankle. If it's what I hope it is, then I might have a plan.

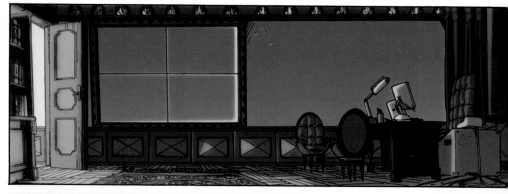

THE BASEMENT SURVEILLANCE MONITOR IS ON. AND THE SHIP CAMERA IS BROADCASTING. IT'S ALL WORKING PERFECTLY.

"Foaly, I'm over Dublin now. When was the last time you updated the Dublin files?"

"Dublin, let's see. Seventy-five... Eighteen seventy-five."

"I got news for you, pony boy. Things have changed just a bit. Just send me an update, would you?"

"That's better. Holly's locator beacon is heading off shore. What's going on?"

"At a guess, sir, I'd say probably a boat or ship."

"Thank you for your genius insight, Foaly. I'm going in."

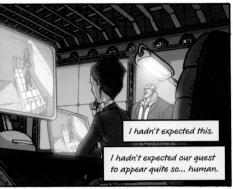

I hadn't expected this.

I hadn't expected our guest to appear quite so... human.

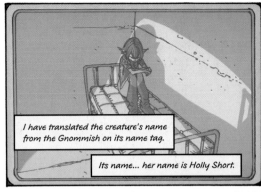

I have translated the creature's name from the Gnommish on its name tag.

Its name... her name is Holly Short.

Until now, they had merely been quarry. Animals to be hunted.

But now, seeing one like this... in obvious discomfort and distress...

I switch off the monitor and recheck the feed from the ship instead. It's nearly time.

Have you activated your shield?

OF COURSE I HAVE. I'M COMPLETELY INVISIBLE TO THE HUMAN EYE. NOT THAT THERE ARE ANY HUMAN EYES... LOOKS DESERTED.

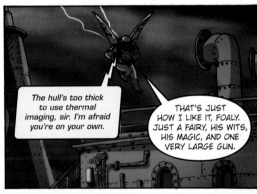

The hull's too thick to use thermal imaging, sir. I'm afraid you're on your own.

THAT'S JUST HOW I LIKE IT, FOALY. JUST A FAIRY, HIS WITS, HIS MAGIC, AND ONE VERY LARGE GUN.

Sir, you know this is almost certainly a trap?

OF COURSE I DO. THAT'S WHY I'M HERE.

I'VE TURNED OFF MY SHIELD SO YOU CAN SEE ME, HUMAN. LOOK IN MY EYES. BELIEVE ME, THERE'S GOING TO BE A RECKONING FOR ALL OF THIS.

"Three..."

IF I WERE YOU, I'D CONCENTRATE ON STAYING ALIVE.

"Two..."

FLY, LITTLE FAIRY. AND TELL YOUR FRIENDS THAT ARTEMIS FOWL THE SECOND SAYS HELLO.

"One..."

"Zero..."

BOOOM!

D'ARVIT!

FOALY, GET ON YOUR COMPUTERS. I WANT TO KNOW EVERYTHING THERE IS TO KNOW ABOUT ONE "ARTEMIS FOWL." AND I WANT TO KNOW IT BEFORE I GET BACK TO BASE.

"There's going to be a reckoning, all right."

Nicknamed "Beetroot" by his staff.

NAME:
Julius Root

CLASSIFICATION:
LEPrecon commander—known for his liking of noxious fungus cigars

BACKGROUND:
A career cop. He has little respect for authority apart from his own. Has commandeered the Atlantean ambassador's shuttle on more than one occasion leading to minor diplomatic incidents. Head of Recon for many decades—a high pressure job given that Recon is a notoriously dangerous posting with a high fatality rate.

WEAPON OF CHOICE:
Multiphase, water-cooled, tri-barreled blaster

KNOWN RELATIONS:
Older brother—Captain Turnball Root CENSORED CENSORED exile

3a.m. Time, I think, for a little chat with our guest.

ARTEMIS? *ARTEMIS!*

HAPTER 6:

SIEGE

ARTEMIS... IT'S YOUR MOTHER.

I feel a lead ball drop in my stomach.

MADAM FOWL SAYS THAT YOUR FATHER IS BACK. SHE SAYS HE'S COME HOME!

Guilt tears at my insides. I've been thinking about our little fairy friends so much that I had given up.

DID YOU SEE HIM, JULIET? WITH YOUR OWN EYES?

NO, ARTEMIS, SIR. I DID HEAR VOICES, THOUGH, FROM HER BEDROOM.

I take the stairs two at a time.

Is it possible?

MOTHER? I'M COMING IN.

Oh...no...

HELLO, PAPA. CAN'T YOU EVEN GIVE YOUR BOY ONE NIGHT OFF? AFTER ALL, IT IS OUR HONEYMOON...

WHAT DO YOU SAY, PAPA? JUST ONE NIGHT OFF, EH?

"Papa"—she thinks I'm my own grandfather... He died over ten years ago. I nod.

I leave her to her fantasies. What else can I do?

My head has been clear for half an hour, but I don't let them know that.

I reach into my boot and find what I'm hoping for. The acorn. Must have slipped in there during the fight.

All I need now is a small patch of earth—then I could restore my powers.

There's nowhere to bury my secret weapon, though. The humans have seen to that.

LOOKING FOR SOMETHING?

The Mud Boy entered the room without a sound. Extraordinary.

WE ARE BOTH FULLY AWARE OF THE RULES HERE. THIS IS MY HOUSE. YOU MUST ABIDE BY MY WISHES. YOUR LAWS, NOT MINE.

OBVIOUSLY, MY WISHES DO NOT INCLUDE BODILY HARM TO MYSELF, OR YOU ATTEMPTING TO LEAVE THIS HOUSE, CAPTAIN SHORT.

HOW DO YOU KNOW...

YOU'RE WEARING A NAME TAG.

BUT THAT'S WRITTEN IN...

GNOMMISH. I KNOW. I'M FLUENT. AS IS EVERYONE ELSE IN MY NETWORK.

My lie hits her hard.

FOWL, YOU'VE NO IDEA WHAT YOU'VE DONE. BRINGING THE WORLDS TOGETHER LIKE THIS COULD MEAN DISASTER FOR US ALL.

"I am not concerned with 'us all,' Captain Short, just myself. And believe me, I will be perfectly fine."

"So what is the master plan, Fowl? Let me guess—world domination?"

NOTHING SO GRAND. JUST RICHES. I'LL BECOME THE WORLD'S FIRST CROSS-SPECIES THIEF AFTER I SEPARATE YOU FROM YOUR HOSTAGE FUND.

WHAT HOSTAGE FUND?

She's struggling to keep her face under control.

YOU TOLD ME ABOUT IT YOURSELF. LOOK AT YOUR ARM. THAT'S WHERE WE ADMINISTERED THE TRUTH SERUM.

YOU'VE ALREADY TOLD US EVERYTHING WE WANTED TO KNOW.

There has been no truth serum, but I cannot afford to reveal the Book as my source of information.

WELL, I CAN'T HAVE TOLD YOU MUCH IN A FEW HOURS.

A FEW HOURS? YOU'VE BEEN HERE FOR THREE DAYS.

WE'VE HAD YOU ON A DRIP FOR OVER SIXTY HOURS... UNTIL WE GOT WHAT WE NEEDED.

This ruse disturbs even me. It feels cruel.

IF YOU KNOW SO MUCH ABOUT US, THEN YOU'LL KNOW WHAT HAPPENS WHEN THEY LOCATE ME. TELL ME, BOY, HAVE YOU EVER MET A TROLL?

NO. NEVER A TROLL.

"You will, Fowl. You will. And when you do, I hope I'm there to see it."

TELL ME WHAT YOU FOUND ON THE HUMAN.

I HACKED INTO INTERPOL. TEN-GIGABYTE FILE. THE FOWLS HAVE BEEN RACKETEERING, SMUGGLING, AND GENERALLY BREAKING EVERY LAW IN THE BOOK FOR GENERATIONS.

SO DO WE HAVE A LOCATION?

THAT'S THE ONE BIT OF GOOD NEWS... FOWL MANOR, A TWO-HUNDRED-ACRE ESTATE ON THE OUTSKIRTS OF DUBLIN. ONLY TWENTY KLICKS FROM HERE.

SO WE COULD MOVE RIGHT NOW AND MAKE IT BEFORE FIRST LIGHT?

YEP. MAYBE SORT THIS WHOLE MESS OUT BEFORE IT GETS OUT OF HAND IN THE RAYS OF THE SUN.

RIGHT. FOALY, I'M GOING ON WITH LIEUTENANT CUDGEON HERE AND THE SQUAD.

YOU ROUND UP THE TECHIES AND FOLLOW US IN THE SHUTTLE. AND BRING THE BIG DISHES. WE'LL TIME-STOP THE ENTIRE ESTATE.

COMMANDER... SOMETHING'S BOTHERING ME. WHY DID THIS HUMAN TELL US WHO HE WAS? HE KNEW WE'D FIND HIM.

MAYBE HE'S NOT AS CLEVER AS HE THINKS HE IS?

HE'S BEEN ONE STEP AHEAD OF US ALL THE WAY, AND I DON'T THINK THAT THIS IS ANY DIFFERENT.

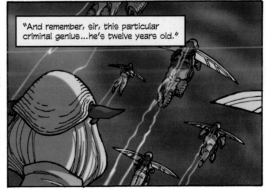

"And remember, sir, this particular criminal genius...he's twelve years old."

EVERYONE, LOCK AND LOAD. *V*-FLIGHT PATTERN. SHIELDS ON.

YOU KNOW WHAT I THINK WE SHOULD DO, JULIUS?

I CAN GUESS.

I THINK WE SHOULD BLAST THE WHOLE PLACE.

WHAT A SURPRISE. YOU WANT TO USE THE BIO-BOMB.

DESTROYS ALL LIVING TISSUE AN LEAVES THE BUILDING STANDING.

ONE BLUE RINSE, AND OU LOSSES ARE MINIMAL

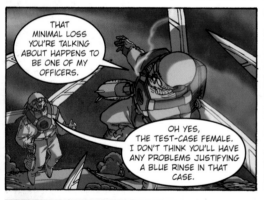

THAT MINIMAL LOSS YOU'RE TALKING ABOUT HAPPENS TO BE ONE OF MY OFFICERS.

OH YES, THE TEST-CASE FEMALE. I DON'T THINK YOU'LL HAVE ANY PROBLEMS JUSTIFYING A BLUE RINSE IN THAT CASE.

SHUT UP OR I'M GONNA RAM THAT BLUE RINSE STRAIGHT INTO THE EMPTY SPACE WHERE YOUR BRAIN SHOULD BE.

CAPTAIN KELP, TAKE YOUR MEN. TWENTY FEET APART. SWEEP THE AREA.

INSULTING ME DOESN'T CHANGE THE FACTS. YOU KNOW WHAT THE BOOK SAYS. WE CANNOT UNDER ANY CIRCUMSTANCES ALLOW THE LOWER ELEMENTS TO BE COMPROMISED.

YOU'VE GOT ONE CHANCE AT A TIME-STOP, JULIUS, DON'T MESS IT UP.

ANYTHING?

NOTHING. ONCE OR TWICE I THOUGHT I SAW A FLICKER, BUT IT TURNED OUT TO BE NOTHING.

NOTHING IS NOTHING. USE THE NEW HIGH-SPEED CINE-CAMERA WE PUT IN. TRY THE AVENUE. I HAVE A FEELING THAT VISITORS ARE ON THE WAY.

STILL NOTHING. THERE'S NO ONE THERE.

FREEZE IT.

WHERE DID THEY SPRING FROM?

THEY'RE SHIELDED. VIBRATING AT A SPEED TOO FAST FOR THE HUMAN EYE TO REGISTER.

I'VE RIGGED THE REMAINS OF CAPTAIN SHORT'S HELMET INTO SOMETHING YOU CAN WEAR.

THIS THING IS EQUIPPED WITH SEVERAL FILTERS. IT STANDS TO REASON THAT ONE OF THEM HAS TO BE ANTISHIELD, SO THAT OUR FRIENDS CAN SEE EACH OTHER.

TIME TO DO WHAT YOU DO BEST. OH, AND BUTLER, I'D PREFER THEM SCARED TO DEAD. IF POSSIBLE.

"This is Captain Trouble Kelp. Retrieval Team One, check in, please."

NEGATIVE ON ONE.

NOTHING CAPTAIN.

ALL CLEAR HERE.

A BIG NEGATORI THERE, TRUBS.

WE'RE IN THE FIELD, CORPORAL. YOU MAY BE MY BROTHER, BUT RANK IS RANK. YOU WILL REFER TO ME AS CAPTAIN KELP.

But Mommy said...

SHUT UP ABOUT MOMMY, WILL YOU! YOU'RE ONLY ON THIS MISSION BECAUSE I REQUESTED YOU.

NOW, START ACTING LIKE A PROFESSIONAL!

Fine, just don't ask me to iron your tunic anymore, will you, Trubs.

ARRKK

WHAT WAS THAT?

SQUAD
CHECK IN...

"One, OK."

"Two, fine."

"Three, bored
but alive."

"Five, approaching the house."

FOUR IS DOWN.
NOBODY PANIC. THE HUMAN
CANNOT SEE US SO IT MUST
HAVE BEEN AN ACCIDENT AS
HE OPENED THE DOOR.

MOVE IN
QUIETLY AND SURROUND
THE TARGET.

"Remember—he cannot see us.
We are completely invisible to him."

EVENING,
GENTLEMEN.

"Oh no."

FREEZE, MUD BOY. JUST GIVE ME A REASON.

THIS ENOUGH REASON?

SLAPPP!

SCARED, CERTAINLY. DEAD? PROBABLY NOT. MISSION ACCOMPLISHED.

AND THAT'S HANDY. ONE OF YOU IS STILL AWAKE.

GULP!

NAME?

GRUB... ER... I MEAN CORPORAL KELP.

WELL, CORPORAL, I HAVE A VERY IMPORTANT MESSAGE FOR YOU TO TAKE BACK TO YOUR COMMANDING OFFICER. ARE YOU LISTENING CAREFULLY?

YOU TELL YOUR COMMANDER THAT THE NEXT TIME I SEE ARMED FORCES COMING IN HERE, THEY'LL BE PICKED OFF BY SNIPER FIRE.

EVEN MORE IMPORTANT, I WANT A NEGOTIATOR SENT IN. SOMEONE WHO CAN ACTUALLY MAKE DECISIONS. GOT IT?

I know they're watching.

The weight of the bed nearly pops my elbows from their sockets.

SMASHH

But it's working.

A satisfying cloud of dust and concrete splinters swirls around my knees.

I hear footsteps outside.

WHAT ARE YOU DOING? TRYING TO KNOCK THE HOUSE DOWN?

I'M HUNGRY! AND I'M TIRED OF WAVING AT THAT STUPID CAMERA. I WANT SOME FOOD.

GET ME SOME FRUIT OR VEGETABLES. AND MAKE SURE THEY'RE WASHED. I DON'T WANT ANY OF YOUR CHEMICAL POISONS IN MY BLOOD.

JUST DON'T GO FORGETTING THE RULES. NO TRYING TO ESCAPE FROM THE HOUSE. AND THERE'S NO NEED TO BREAK UP THE FURNITURE.

The thing about Fairy bonds is that they have to be very precise.

Just saying there was no need to do a thing does not forbid it.

And while I may be forbidden to escape from this house, that doesn't mean I can't get out of this cell.

The camera in Mother's room is working now.

It feels almost like spying, but it is for her own good.

HOW'S OUR PRISONER?

ANY PROBLEMS?

NOTHING MAJOR. TRICKY LITTLE BLIGHTERS THOUGH. THOSE LITTLE BATONS PACK QUITE A PUNCH.

CAPTAIN SHORT IS GOING A BIT STIR-CRAZY, I THINK. BANGING HER BED AROUND.

IT'S UNDERSTANDABLE. IMAGINE HOW FRUSTRATED SHE MUST BE. MAYBE SHE'S TRYING TO TUNNEL HER WAY OUT.

WELL, DON'T WORRY, OLD FRIEND. THIS ENTIRE ESTATE IS BUILT ON A BED OF LIMESTONE.

"Nothing could tunnel its way in or out of here."

SO, FOALY, ARE WE GOOD TO GO YET?

COMMANDER, THIS ISN'T JUST A MATTER OF PRESSING THE "ON" BUTTON. CREATING A TIME-STOP IS A DELICATE PROCEDURE THAT HAS TO BE PERFORMED WITH THE UTMOST PRECISION.

IT'S NOT EASY BEING AN UNAPPRECIATED GENIUS.

OK, WE'RE READY.

ABOUT TIME, TOO. RIGHT, FLIP THE SWITCH.

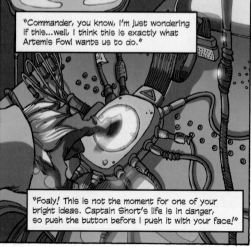

"Commander, you know, I'm just wondering if this...well, I think this is exactly what Artemis Fowl wants us to do."

"Foaly! This is not the moment for one of your bright ideas. Captain Short's life is in danger, so push the button before I push it with your face!"

SKRAKRUMP!

YOU'VE GOT YOUR TIME-STOP, COMMANDER.

GOOD WORK, FOALY.

FSHAMMM

FSHAMMM

YOU HAVE EIGHT HOURS.

I KNOW HOW MUCH TIME I HAVE, CUDGEON. DON'T YOU HAVE WORK TO DO?

NOW YOU MENTION IT, I DO HAVE A BIO-BOMB TO ARM.

DO WHAT YOU FEEL YOU HAVE TO. BUT BE PREPARED TO BACK IT UP AT TRIBUNAL. IF THIS ONE GOES WRONG, BELIEVE ME, HEADS ARE GOING TO ROLL.

INDEED, AND I'M GOING TO MAKE SURE THAT MY HEAD IS NOT ONE OF THEM.

ALL RIGHT, FOALY, I'M THE ONE GOING IN TO "NEGOTIATE" WITH THE MUD BOY. WHAT HAVE YOU GOT FOR ME?

FIRST A TIP: WATCH OUT FOR CUDGEON. IF HE GETS A CHANCE TO STAB YOU IN THE BACK, HE WON'T WASTE A SECOND.

YOU'RE WRONG ABOUT CUDGEON. HE'S A GOOD OFFICER. A BIT EAGER, MAYBE, BUT WHEN THE TIME COMES, HE'LL DO THE RIGHT THING.

THE RIGHT THING FOR HIMSELF, MAYBE. I DON'T THINK HOLLY IS EXACTLY TOP OF HIS PRIORITY LIST, IS SHE?

CUDGEON WILL DO WHAT I TELL HIM.

TIME-STOPS ARE HARD GOING. YOUR BODY GETS TIRED, BUT YOUR MIND WON'T LET YOU FALL ASLEEP. WE *ALL* NEED TO WORK TOGETHER.

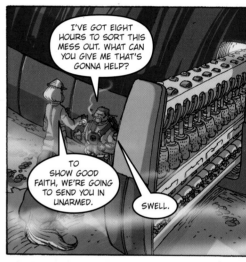

I'VE GOT EIGHT HOURS TO SORT THIS MESS OUT. WHAT CAN YOU GIVE ME THAT'S GONNA HELP?

TO SHOW GOOD FAITH, WE'RE GOING TO SEND YOU IN UNARMED.

SWELL.

"Of course, we'll fit you with an iris-cam in your eye so we can record visuals and audio of the meeting."

TALK TO THE FOWL BOY. FEEL HIM OUT. SEE WHAT HE WANTS.

LET'S HOPE HE MAKES A MISTAKE. AND SOON.

My watch has stopped. The picture on CNN has frozen...

They've done it. Just like the Book said they would. They've stopped time.

Time to check out a theory. Time to send Juliet upstairs with a sleeping pill for mother.

IT SEEMS, SIR, THAT WE ARE ABOUT TO HAVE A GUEST.

Best sinister face. Evil, highly intelligent, and determined. Don't forget determined.

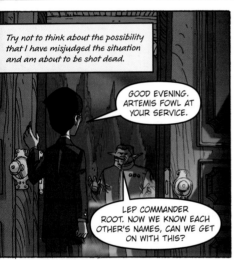

Try not to think about the possibility that I have misjudged the situation and am about to be shot dead.

GOOD EVENING. ARTEMIS FOWL AT YOUR SERVICE.

LEP COMMANDER ROOT. NOW WE KNOW EACH OTHER'S NAMES, CAN WE GET ON WITH THIS?

WHY DON'T YOU STEP OUTSIDE, WHERE I CAN SEE YOU?

WHERE I COULD BE SNATCHED AND USED TO TRADE? PLEASE, COMMANDER ROOT, EITHER RAISE YOUR GAME OR SEND SOMEONE AT LEAST SLIGHTLY INTELLIGENT.

HERE IS THE SITUATION AS I SEE IT.

I HAVE THE MEANS TO EXPOSE YOUR SUBTERRANEAN EXISTENCE, AND YOU ARE POWERLESS TO STOP ME.

SO, BASICALLY, WHATEVER I ASK FOR IS A SMALL PRICE TO PAY.

YOU THINK YOU CAN JUST PUT ALL THIS INFORMATION OUT OVER THE INTERNET?

NOT WITH YOUR TIME-STOP IN EFFECT, NO.

WELL, IF YOU KNOW ABOUT THE TIME-STOP, THEN YOU MUST ALSO KNOW THAT YOU ARE COMPLETELY CUT OFF FROM THE OUTSIDE WORLD. YOU ARE POWERLESS.

LET'S SAVE SOME TIME HERE.

I GROW WEARY OF YOUR CLUMSY BLUFFS.

I KNOW THAT IN THE CASE OF AN ABDUCTION, THE LEP WILL FIRST SEND IN A CRACK RETRIEVAL TEAM.

EXCUSE ME WHILE I TITTER. CRACK TEAM? HONESTLY A CUB SCOUT PATROL ARMED WITH WATER PISTOLS COULD HAVE DEFEATED THEM.

THE NEXT STEP IN A TIME-STOP IS NEGOTIATION. IF THAT FAILS, THEN A BIO-BOMB IS DETONATED.

SO, LET'S HAVE IT. WHAT ARE YOUR DEMANDS?

ONE DEMAND. SINGULAR.

YOU CAN'T BE SERIOUS. DON'T YOU SEE? YOU CAN'T WIN. EITHER YOU GIVE US BACK CAPTAIN SHORT OR WE'LL BE FORCED TO KILL YOU.

I DON'T THINK SO, COMMANDER.

YOU SEE, I KNOW HOW TO ESCAPE THE TIME-FIELD.

IMPOSSIBLE. IT CAN'T BE DONE...

OH YES IT CAN. AND I HAVEN'T BEEN WRONG YET.

I'LL HAVE TO THINK ABOUT THIS.

YOU DO THAT. BUT REMEMBER THIS, NONE OF YOUR RACE HAS PERMISSION TO ENTER HERE WHILE I'M ALIVE.

FOALY, DID YOU GET ALL THAT?

THIS MUD BOY'S A SLIPPERY CUSTOMER, ALL RIGHT. BUT HE'S MAKING ONE BASIC MISTAKE.

THIS FOWL PERSON SEEMS TO KNOW ALL OF OUR RULES, SO MAYBE IT'S TIME WE BROKE A FEW.

NAME:
Time-stops

BACKGROUND:
Fairies have been stopping time for millennia. Time-stops were traditionally
initiated by five elfin warlocks who would form a pentagram around the target
and spread an enchanted enclosure over it, temporarily stopping time inside.
This was fine as far as it went, provided the warlocks didn't have to use the
bathroom. Many a siege was lost because an elf had one glass of wine too many.

RECENT DEVELOPMENTS:
LEP technical genius, Foaly, is responsible for what we recognize as the modern
time-stop. With humans developing satellite communication, today's time-stops
need to be fine-tuned and precise. Foaly introduced the idea of warlocks
storing their magic in lithium batteries—a move greatly resisted by powerful
warlock unions at the time. Foaly then engineered a network of mobile receiver
dishes that could be positioned around the designated area. These developments
mean that sieges can now be extended for up to eight hours.

Bio-bombs—often used by the LEP
in conjunction with time-stops. The
bio-bomb kills all living things in a set
radius, but leaves all other material
intact. The radioactive element used
in the core is solinium 2, which has a
half-life of fourteen seconds.

HAVEN CITY.

A POLICE HOLDING CELL.

CHAPTER 7:

MULCH

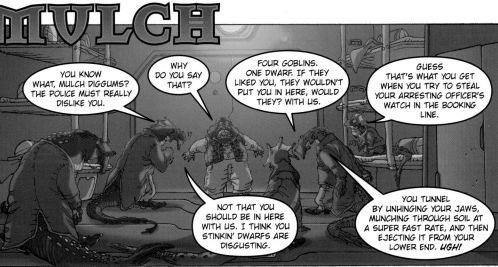

YOU KNOW WHAT, MULCH DIGGUMS? THE POLICE MUST REALLY DISLIKE YOU.

WHY DO YOU SAY THAT?

FOUR GOBLINS. ONE DWARF. IF THEY LIKED YOU, THEY WOULDN'T PUT YOU IN HERE, WOULD THEY? WITH US.

GUESS THAT'S WHAT YOU GET WHEN YOU TRY TO STEAL YOUR ARRESTING OFFICER'S WATCH IN THE BOOKING LINE.

NOT THAT YOU SHOULD BE IN HERE WITH US. I THINK YOU STINKIN' DWARFS ARE DISGUSTING.

YOU TUNNEL BY UNHINGING YOUR JAWS, MUNCHING THROUGH SOIL AT A SUPER FAST RATE, AND THEN EJECTING IT FROM YOUR LOWER END. *UGH!*

I DON'T WANT ANY TROUBLE.

I BET YOU DON'T. WHICH IS A SHAME. FOR YOU, I MEAN.

YOU DWARFS DON'T LIKE FIRE MUCH, DO YOU?

GECK GACK, OR UR GREND GEDDS IT!

YOU CAN'T GET US ALL, STUMPY. READY, BOYS?

YOU GOBLINS, PUT 'EM OUT.

SPIT OUT THE PRISONER.

I'M NOT SURE I'VE EVER SAID THAT BEFORE.

IT'S YOUR LUCKY DAY, MULCH DIGGUMS. SEEMS COMMANDER ROOT WANTS YOU ON THE SURFACE.

JULIUS? WANTS ME?

HEY, HANG ON, ISN'T IT DAYLIGHT BY NOW? I'LL BURN.

IT AIN'T DAYLIGHT WHERE YOU'RE GOING, PAL. WHERE YOU'RE GOING IT AIN'T ANYTHING.

IS HE READY?

I HAVE A NAME, YOU KNOW, JULIUS.

HE'S READY. WIRED WITH AN IRIS-CAM AND SET UP FOR SOUND, TOO.

GETTING INTO THE HOUSE ISN'T A PROBLEM FOR YOU.

YOU'VE ALREADY LOST YOUR MAGIC BECAUSE BREAKING AND ENTERING IS WHAT YOU DO FOR A SO-CALLED LIVING.

I WANT YOU TO TUNNEL IN THERE AND FIND OUT HOW THIS FOWL PERSON KNOWS SO MUCH ABOUT US.

AND IF POSSIBLE, FIND CAPTAIN SHORT AND SEE IF YOU CAN HELP HER.

I DON'T LIKE IT. OUTSIDE, I SMELLED LIMESTONE. SOLID ROCK FOUNDATION.

THERE MIGHT NOT BE A WAY IN.

I'VE DONE A SCAN. THE ORIGINAL BUILDING IS BUILT TOTALLY ON ROCK, BUT SOME OF THE LATER EXTENSIONS STRAY ONTO CLAY.

GOOD LUCK, MULCH.

YOU KNOW, I'VE NEVER ACTUALLY SEEN A DWARF TUNNELING BEFORE.

SPLATTT!

THAT SMELLS SO BAD...

"And don't you even think about trying to escape, convict! Remember, Foaly and I are watching you. The iris-cam shows us everything."

JULIUS? CAN YOU HEAR ME? I'M IN.

We hear you loud and clear.

DOOR'S LOCKED, BUT THE HUMANS HAVEN'T MADE A LOCK THAT CAN'T BE PICKED BY DWARF HAIR.

THREE CAMERAS ON THE CORRIDOR. NINETY-SECOND SWEEP. NO WAY THROUGH.

"Foaly here. Adjusting the iris-cam."

HANDY...

"OK, Mulch. It's a simple video network. I'm going to broadcast a loop of the last ten seconds to every camera from our dishes. Count to three, then move it."

WHATEVER YOU DID MUST HAVE WORKED.

I TELL YOU, JULIUS, AFTER ALL THAT TUNNELING, I GOT A VERY BAD CASE OF DWARF GAS BUILDING UP DOWN BELOW.

You are a disgusting individual, Diggums!

HEY, THERE'S A VASE IN HERE THAT LOOKS...

You're not in there to rob the place, Diggums. You're there to find out how Fowl knows so much about us.

THERE'S AN INTERESTING ROOM HERE, FOALY. MUST BE IMPORTANT. IT'S GOT THREE HIDDEN CAMERAS. I NEED TO KNOW EXACTLY WHERE THEY'RE POINTING. CAN YOU HELP?

This may sting a bit...

NOT BEHIND THE PICTURE. OH PLEASE.

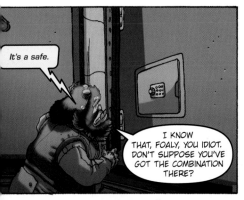

THERE'S ANOTHER SAFE HERE. IT'S MUCH SMALLER... HIDDEN IN THE PAINTING FRAME ITSELF.

It's lead-lined. X-rays are no good, so you're on your own.

This is Root. Hurry it up, convict. Your time is running out.

CLICKKK

YOU'RE TELLING ME. THIS GAS PROBLEM'S KILLING ME.

I reboot the system and purge the loop.

Everything changes.

Suddenly there's some grotesque thing in the safe room. And it's already opening the secret compartment. I decide to leave that to Butler.

At least Holly's stopped banging her bed up and down. Now she's kneeling on the floor like she's...oh no.

Juliet! Don't go into Holly's room! **Do not go in!**

I see it. A sliver of brown among the gray.

I RETURN YOU TO THE EARTH, AND CLAIM THE GIFT THAT IS MY RIGHT.

UGH...

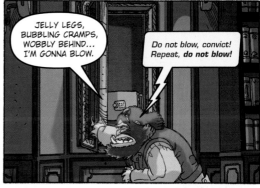

I'M COMING IN NOW, FAIRY GIRL, SO IF YOU'RE DOING ANYTHING EMBARRASSING, PLEASE STOP IT.

WHERE ARE...

WHY DON'T YOU TAKE OFF THOSE GLASSES, JULIET? THEY REALLY DON'T SUIT YOU.

I'LL TAKE OFF THESE GLASSES. THEY REALLY DON'T SUIT ME.

THAT'S BETTER. NOW I'VE GOT A FEW QUESTIONS FOR YOU.

Get a move on, convict, before that Mud Man gets up and rearranges your innards.

HOW MANY PEOPLE ARE THERE IN THE HOUSE?

THREE. ME, AND BUTLER, AND, OF COURSE, ARTEMIS.

MRS. FOWL WAS HERE, BUT NOT ANYMORE.

nearly ask what she means, but I decide it's not worth it.

HAS ANYONE ELSE BEEN HERE? ANYONE LIKE ME?

THERE WAS ONE LITTLE MAN. SHOUTED MOST OF THE TIME AND SMOKED A SMELLY CIGAR.

Root.

NOW, JULIET I WANT YOU TO SIT HERE AND NOT LEAVE THIS ROOM, OK? THERE'S A NEW TV ON THIS WALL SHOWING JUST WHAT YOU LIKE TO WATCH. CAN YOU SEE IT?

And it was all going so well.

MULCH DIGGUMS. I WASN'T EXPECTING TO SEE YOU HERE.

CAPTAIN SHORT! WELL, JULIUS HAD A DIRTY JOB, AND SOMEONE HAD TO DO IT.

I GET IT. YOU'VE ALREADY LOST YOUR MAGIC. SMART. WHAT DID YOU FIND OUT?

SHE'S ALIVE.

SHE'S ALIVE.

THIS WAS IN HIS SAFE.

A COPY OF THE *BOOK!*

NO WONDER WE'RE IN A FIX. WE MUST HAVE BEEN PLAYING RIGHT INTO HIS HANDS ALL ALONG.

MULCH, I CAN'T GO WITH YOU. I'M UNDER ORDERS NOT TO LEAVE THE HOUSE.

YOU MAGICAL TYPES AND YOUR RITUALS. YOU HAVE NO IDEA HOW LIBERATING IT IS TO BE RID OF ALL THAT MUMBO-JUMBO.

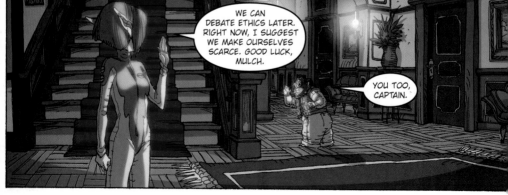

WE CAN DEBATE ETHICS LATER. RIGHT NOW, I SUGGEST WE MAKE OURSELVES SCARCE. GOOD LUCK, MULCH.

YOU TOO, CAPTAIN.

Things are not good.

The manor's security has been compromised by an unsightly creature in leather pants.

The safe room has been blown apart by some sort of unwelcome fairy flatulence.

The same gaseous anomaly has also rendered Butler unconscious for a time.

And the People have retrieved the copy of the Book from the hidden safe.

...will have to dig very deep to uncover the good in this particular scenario.

I take several deep breaths. I focus. I find my chi.

Just as Butler always taught me.

I realize... I realize that what has happened means very little to the overall strategies of either side.

The People have recovered only one of several copies I have made of the Book.

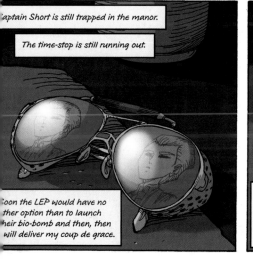

Captain Short is still trapped in the manor.

The time-stop is still running out.

Soon the LEP would have no other option than to launch their bio-bomb and then, then I will deliver my coup de grace.

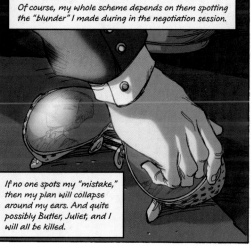

Of course, my whole scheme depends on them spotting the "blunder" I made during in the negotiation session.

If no one spots my "mistake," then my plan will collapse around my ears. And quite possibly Butler, Juliet, and I will all be killed.

NAME:
Mulch Diggums

CLASSIFICATION:
Dwarf, Career criminal

BACKGROUND:
Criminal individual who decided early in life that mining was not for him
and resolved to put his talents to other uses. Convicted several times for
Digging and Entering. Entering the property of Mud People without their
permission meant that Mulch forfeited his fairy magic long ago. Like all
dwarves, Mulch is terrified of fire.

CRIMINAL RECORD:
Has spent the last three hundred years going in and out of prison

ARRESTING OFFICERS:
Julius Root—eight times. Holly Short—at least once—see "Fei Fei" case file

KNOWN ALIASES:
Lance Digger, the Grouch

KNOWN RELATIONS:
His cousin—Nord

WEAPON OF CHOICE:
His powerful jaws

Mulch Diggums is the only
fairy ever to break into the
infamous Koboi Laboratories
and survive.

LEP MOBILE HQ-FOWL ESTATE.

WE HAVE HIM! FOWL HAS MADE A FATAL MISTAKE!

IT'S ELEMENTARY GRAMMAR.

But remember this, none of your race has permission to enter here while I'm alive.

THE HUMAN SPECIFICALLY STATED THAT ENTRY WAS FORBIDDEN AS LONG AS HE WAS ALIVE. AND THAT'S TANTAMOUNT TO AN INVITATION WHEN HE'S DEAD.

HUMMM, I DON'T KNOW...THE INVITATION IS IMPLIED AT BEST.

COME ON, JULIUS, HOW MUCH MORE DO YOU NEED? ONCE FOWL IS DEAD, THE DOOR IS WIDE OPEN. HE SAID IT HIMSELF. THIS IS HOLLY'S LIFE WE'RE TALKING ABOUT.

ONE, YOU'RE RIGHT. TWO, I'M GOING TO RUN WITH IT. THREE, WELL DONE, YOU TWO. AND FOUR, IF YOU EVER CALL ME "JULIUS" AGAIN, FOALY, YOU'LL BE EATING YOUR OWN HOOVES FOR BREAKFAST.

SO WE SEND IN THE GOLD. THEY SEND OUT HOLLY, WE BLUE-RINSE THE PLACE AND THEN STROLL IN TO RECLAIM THE RANSOM. NICE.

FOALY, GET ME A LINE TO THE COUNCIL. I NEED TO GET APPROVAL FOR THAT GOLD.

ER...SIR. THERE'S SOMETHING OUTSIDE I THINK YOU REALLY, REALLY, NEED TO SEE...

CHAPTER 8:
TROLL

I have a plan. Of sorts.

Sneak around a bit. Sneak around a bit more. Reclaim some fairy weaponry.

Wreak havoc.

If several million pounds' worth of property damage happens to ensue, well that would be a bonus.

Now I've completed the Ritual, I'm running hot.

Truth is, I haven't felt this good in years.

Footsteps.

Thundering footsteps.

JULIET!

He must have just spotted her under the effect of the *mesmer*.

GOOD EVENING, CAPTAIN SHORT.

AT THE RISK OF SOUNDING CLICHÉD, I'VE BEEN EXPECTING YOU.

YOU ARE OF COURSE STILL BOUND BY THE PROMISES MADE EARLIER TONIGHT. SO, BASICALLY OUR SITUATION HASN'T CHANGED.

Where is it?

I see the equipment.

If I can get a helmet on, then he won't be able to give me any more orders. I'll be safe behind the reflective visor.

YOU ARE STILL MY HOSTAGE.

...on revolving frequencies. Holly, if you can hear me, take cover. This is Foaly, broadcasting on revolving frequencies.

I say again they are sending in a troll to secure your release. Take cover!

IT'S NOT POLITE, YOU KNOW, IGNORING YOUR HOST.

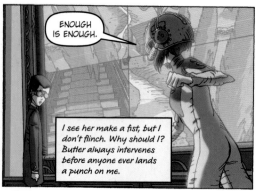

ENOUGH IS ENOUGH.

I see her make a fist, but I don't flinch. Why should I? Butler always intervenes before anyone ever lands a punch on me.

Butler.

THWOKK

YOU HIT ME.

AND THERE'S PLENTY MORE WHERE THAT CAME FROM. SO STAY RIGHT WHERE YOU ARE, IF YOU KNOW WHAT'S GOOD FOR YOU.

tried the doorknob, and got a scorched palm for my trouble.

Sealed.

Captain Short must have blasted it with her weapon.

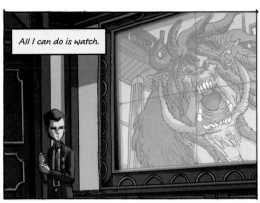

All I can do is watch.

Butler is expecting a military attack rather than the world's most perfect killing machine.

On any other day, Butler would be halfway up the staircase by now.

On any other day, he wouldn't have Juliet to protect.

The creature is on him in seconds.

Butler gets two shots into the creature's chest, but it just keeps coming.

All I can do is watch.

It takes me less than forty seconds to put the wings on and get them working after Fowl's tinkering, but it's already too late for the male.

I drop into a controlled dive. All this to save a human.

I've gone section eight without a doubt

My gun's good for maybe one shot. I need to get close.

The pain hits me hard.

Curved nails scrape my helmet

The troll squeezes the breath out of me.

This isn't going well.

This is Root. Use your helmet lights, Holly! Lights!!

I look the troll straight in the eyes and press the butto

Four-hundred watts of light fail to come on.

I picked up a helmet cannibalized by the humans. Thank you, Artemis Fow

Lights are offline, so I hit the troll with the only weapon I have left.

My head.

The blow has no effect...

...except for connecting two strands of wire somewhere in the helmet, sending power flooding to one of the lights.

GRRRRRRR

It grabs me and throws me hard.

I feel a rib puncture my lung.

My arm snaps on impact with the floor.

It hurts, but my magic should kick in any second.

Amazingly, the human isn't dead.

A desperate dogged pulse forces blood through his smashed limbs.

Heal.

The human gets up looking for a fight. I try to warn him, but the magic hasn't reinflated my crushed lung yet.

Butler is alive.

STEP AWAY FROM THE FEMALE. EASY NOW.

Idiot. The human is trying to engage the troll in macho repartee.

No, wait. The words aren't important. It's the tone. Calm, soothing. Like a trainer with a spooked unicorn.

NICE AND EASY THERE, BIG FELLOW.

THWAKK

KRAKKK

LOOK WHAT I FOUND.

BAM BAM BAM

NO ONE TOUCHES MY SISTER.

RRRRAAAAA.

KLUDD

KRAKK

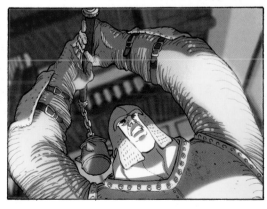

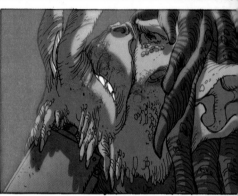

NAME:
Trolls

CLASSIFICATION:
The most deadly of the deep-tunnel creatures. Trolls wander around the labyrinth of tunnels under the surface of the earth. Any living thing they encounter is likely to end up on the menu.

ENCOUNTERED WHEN:
Occasionally a troll finds its way into the shaft of a pressure elevator. Usually the concentrated air current incinerates them, but in rare instances one survives and is blasted all the way to the surface. Surface exposure to light always drives the troll crazy, sending it on a rampage. The first troll to be captured alive in over a century was caught by Captain Holly Short during its surface rampage in southern Italy.

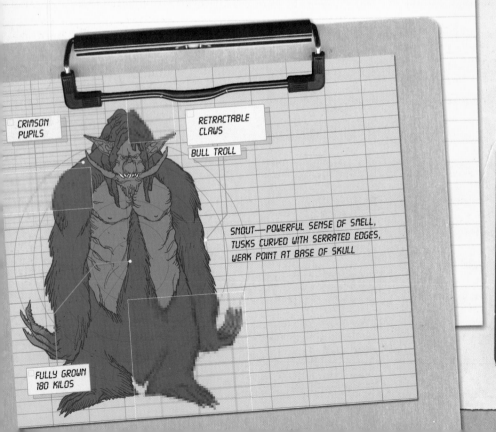

CRIMSON PUPILS

RETRACTABLE CLAWS

BULL TROLL

SNOUT—POWERFUL SENSE OF SMELL, TUSKS CURVED WITH SERRATED EDGES, WEAK POINT AT BASE OF SKULL

FULLY GROWN 180 KILOS

I saw it all and I appreciate now, perhaps for the first time, everything that Butler does for me.

CHAPTER 9:
ACE IN THE HOLE

COMMANDER ROOT, I PRESUME YOU ARE MONITORING ALL CHANNELS. IN SPITE OF YOUR ATTEMPTED BETRAYAL, I AM STILL WILLING TO NEGOTIATE.

That troll had nothing to do with me, Fowl. It was done against my wishes.

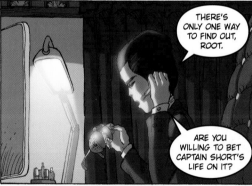

THE FACT IS, IT WAS DONE. AND BY THE LEP.

HERE IS MY ULTIMATUM. YOU HAVE THIRTY MINUTES TO SEND IN THE GOLD. IF YOU DO NOT, I WILL REFUSE TO RELEASE CAPTAIN SHORT.

FURTHERMORE, I WILL NOT TAKE HER WITH ME WHEN I ESCAPE THE TIME-FIELD, LEAVING HER TO BE DISINTEGRATED BY YOUR OWN BIO-BOMB.

Don't be a fool, human. You're deluding yourself. There is no way to escape the time-field.

THERE'S ONLY ONE WAY TO FIND OUT, ROOT.

ARE YOU WILLING TO BET CAPTAIN SHORT'S LIFE ON IT?

No. You'll have your gold, Fowl.

So the bait has been taken.

No doubt LEP analysts have discovered my "accidental" invitation to enter the house in the event of my death.

Their plan is simple. The fairies will part with their precious gold, because they believe that after they have bio-bombed me, they will be able to stroll into Fowl Manor and take back their gold. Of course, they're quite wrong.

I hope.

Butler uses his Sig Sauer to undo Captain Short's handiwork and open the door.

NICE WORK DOWNSTAIRS, BUTLER.

THANK YOU, ARTEMIS. WE WERE IN TROUBLE THERE. IF IT HADN'T BEEN FOR THE CAPTAIN...

YES, I SAW. HEALING. ONE OF THE FAIRY ARTS. I WONDER WHY SHE DID IT?

I WONDER TOO. WE CERTAINLY DIDN'T DESERVE IT.

Butler is a man of great honor. He does not find kidnapping innocents easy.

KEEP THE FAITH, OLD FRIEND. IN LESS THAN AN HOUR, CAPTAIN SHORT WILL BE BACK WITH HER PEOPLE. NO HARM WILL BEFALL HER. YOU HAVE MY WORD.

AND JULIET? IS THERE ANY DANGER TO MY SISTER?

NO. NO DANGER.

SO OUR ADVERSARIES ARE JUST GOING TO GIVE US THE GOLD AND WALK AWAY?

NOT EXACTLY. THE SECOND CAPTAIN SHORT IS CLEAR, THEY PLAN TO BIO-BOMB THE MANOR AND KILL US ALL.

Butler opens his mouth to ask a question, but changes his mind.

I TRUST YOU, ARTEMIS.

And I cannot let him down.

If the humans are expecting to be paid in gold, then I know what's coming.

Their utter destruction.

There is no doubt in my mind that Fowl is a danger to every civilized fairy under the world.

But the girl, Juliet, is an innocent. She deserves a chance.

HAVE YOU TOLD THEM?

TOLD THEM WHAT?

DON'T THINK I'VE FORGOTTEN ABOUT THE MESMERIZING, FAIRY. YOU MADE ME LOOK LIKE A FOOL.

DON'T PLAY DUMB, FOWL. YOU KNOW WHAT I'M TALKING ABOUT.

YES, CAPTAIN SHORT, I DO. THE BIO-BOMB DO NOT UPSET YOURSELF. EVERYTHING IS PROCEEDING ACCORDING TO PLAN.

ACCORDING TO PLAN?

WAS GETTING HALF THE HOUSE BLOWN UP PART OF THE PLAN? AND BUTLER ALMOST GETTING KILLED? WAS THAT ALL PART OF THE PLAN?

NO. I ADMIT, THE TROLL WAS A BIT OF A BLIP...

I resist the urge to punch him again. Just

LISTEN TO REASON, FOR HEAVEN'S SAKE. YOU CANNOT ESCAPE THE TIME-FIELD. IT HAS NEVER BEEN DONE.

IF ARTEMIS SAYS IT CAN BE DONE, THEN IT CAN.

AND YOU'RE WILLING TO RISK THE LIFE OF YOUR SISTER OUT OF LOYALTY TO A FELON?

ARTEMIS IS NO FELON, MISS. HE'S A GENIUS.

It's hard to tell, but I think he believes it

"Foaly, it that what I think it is?"

"Holly's coming out! And with half the gold?"

YOU GAVE IT BACK?

ABOUT HALF. I FELT WE OWED THE CAPTAIN SOMETHING. FOR SERVICES RENDERED.

No need to talk about the wish.

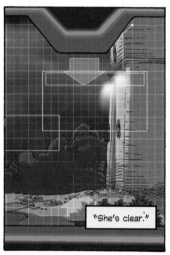

"She's clear."

NOW WE SHOULD CELEBRATE. SOME CHAMPAGNE, I THINK.

"Stand by, Foaly."

I KNOW I'M UNDERAGE, BUT I'M SURE MOTHER WOULDN'T MIND JUST THIS ONCE.

"Launch it."

YOU KNOW I LOVE YOU, DON'T YOU, SIS?

WHAT?

VWOOOSH

NOTHING.

YOU'RE SO EMOTIONAL FOR A BODYGUARD.

YOU NEED US TO DRINK THIS, DON'T YOU, ARTEMIS?

YES, BUTLER, I DO.

VWOOOSH

The tranquilizer hits immediately.

BA-DOOOOM

For a moment, I wonder if maybe, just maybe, they'll survive.

Then I remember the technology at Foaly's fingertips, and I realize the humans are as good as dead.

Insects shrivel.

Inside the manor, flowers wither.

Fish die in their tanks.

Not one cubic millimeter was spared.

Artemis Fowl and his cohorts could not have escaped.

For some reason, I mourn his passing.

Going back in and identifying the bodies doesn't appeal to me at all, but I know it's my duty.

There's also the small matter of getting the rest of the gold back.

The house is a cradle of death.

Behind those medieval walls lie the bodies of a million insects, and under its floors the cooling corpses of spiders and mice.

Radiation negative. No thermals either. It's clean.

I DON'T FEEL SO GOOD...

Then I realize what's happening. It's the magic. It has to be. They can't enter the house until Fowl is dead. Somehow he's done it. Fowl is alive.

UGH...

I go on alone. I have to be certain.

If there is a body, it'll be with the gold.

There's nothing here. Artemis Fowl has escaped the time-stop.

He has done the impossible.

NEGATIVE ON ANY BODIES, SIR. HE'S ESCAPED. BUT I HAVE FOUND THE REST OF THE RANSOM.

Leave it alone, Holly. You know the rules. If he's still alive, then he's won and the gold is his to keep.

We have been beaten by a human. And an adolescent human at that.

Fowl is the winner this time. But I bet he'll be back.

And when he does return, I'll be waiting for him with a smile and a very, very big gun.

"Artemis?"

FATHER?

The word feels strange in my mouth. Unused. Rusty.

EXPLAIN YOURSELF, ARTEMIS. NOW.

I think I've just been given an order.

I DIDN'T TELL YOU OR JULIET ABOUT THE SLEEPING PILLS BECAUSE YOU'D FIGHT THEM.

IT'S ONLY NATURAL. AND IT WAS IMPERATIVE TO THE PLAN THAT WE GO TO SLEEP IMMEDIATELY.

"THE PLAN"?

THE TIME-FIELD WAS THE KEY TO THIS WHOLE AFFAIR. THAT'S WHY THE LEP HAVE BEEN UNBEATABLE UP TO NOW.

I HAD TO THINK OF A WAY TO ESCAPE THE TIME-FIELD. I TRAWLED THROUGH THE FAIRIES' OWN SACRED BOOK, BUT THERE WAS NOTHING. NOT A CLUE.

THEN I THOUGHT ABOUT THE OLD FAIRY STORIES WHERE PEOPLE FELL ASLEEP AND WOKE UP TO FIND THE FAIRIES HAD CLEANED THEIR HOUSE OR MADE THEM SHOES.

THAT'S WHEN I REALIZED...

IN THE STORIES, NO ONE EVER WAKES UP AT THE WRONG MOMENT. WHATEVER YOUR STATE OF CONSCIOUSNESS GOING INTO A TIME-STOP, THAT'S HOW YOU STAY. YOU CAN NEITHER WAKE UP OR FALL SLEEP.

THE FAIRY MAGIC WORKED TO KEEP OUR CONSCIOUSNESS IMPRISONED.

THE WAY TO ESCAPE AND SLIP OUT OF THE TIME-FIELD WAS TO SIMPLY FALL ASLEEP.

YOU RISKED AN AWFUL LOT ON A THEORY, ARTEMIS.

NOT JUST A THEORY. AFTER ALL, WE HAD A TEST SUBJECT WHO DID SLIP OUT OF THE TIME-FIELD WHEN SHE TOOK SLEEPING PILLS...

ANGELINE...

WE COULD NOT FALL ASLEEP NATURALLY IN THE TIME-FIELD, SO I ADMINISTERED US ALL A DOSE OF MOTHER'S PILLS. SIMPLE.

YOU CUT IT PRETTY FINE, THOUGH, ARTEMIS. ANOTHER MINUTE AND...

AGREED. LESSON LEARNED.

AM I FORGIVEN?

YES, ARTEMIS. ALL IS FORGIVEN.

I remember Mother. And the millions I gave up for a wish.

I feel gullible beyond belief. Why would Captain Short keep her promise?

There's a noise by the door.

Butler has his Sig Sauer ready before I can even open my mouth to speak.

ARTEMIS, GET BEHIND ME.

I do not know why, but suddenly I have faith that he won't need it.

MORNING, ARTY.

WELL...?

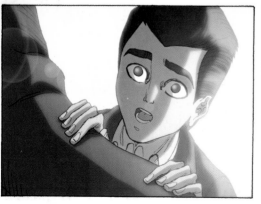

...DON'T I GET A HUG?

Her embrace is warm and strong.

I feel like a boy again.

I'M SORRY, ARTY. I HAVEN'T BEEN MYSELF FOR THE LAST FEW MONTHS. BUT THINGS ARE GOING TO CHANGE. TIME FOR US TO STOP LIVING IN THE PAST.

My mind is racing. Now that Mother is back, my life is going to change. (We're going to have to explain what happened to the entrance hall, for one thing.)

If my plans are going to escape Mother's attention, then they will have to be even more devious than usual.

I tell Butler that in the future we will restrict ourselves to more tasteful ventures.

I can't promise they'll all be legal, though....

Adapted from the novel *Artemis Fowl*.

Text copyright © 2007 by Eoin Colfer
Illustrations copyright © 2007 by Giovanni Rigano
Fact file art elements by Megan Noller Holt

Printed in the United States of America
First Edition
10 9 8 7 6 5 4 3
Library of Congress Cataloging-in-Publication Data on file.
ISBN-13: 978-0-7868-4881-2
ISBN-10: 0-7868-4881-2 (hardcover)
ISBN-13: 978-0-7868-4882-9
ISBN-10: 0-7868-4882-0 (paperback)

Visit www.artemisfowl.com and www.hyperionbooksforchildren.com